MYTHS AND LEGENDS

MONSTERS
BEASTS
& DRAGONS

CONTENTS

MONSTERS OF THE WORLD

All cultures in the world believe in good and evil. The mythology of each culture has a rich tradition of tales relating the powers and weaknesses of monsters and beasts. A monster or a beast was generally thought to be hideous and scary to look at, and were usually depicted as opposed to the gods and heroes in legends.

The Chimera of Greek mythology was believed to have had the heads of a goat and a lion, and a snake for its tail

BEST OF BOTH WORLDS

Some monsters were part human and part animal. They usually had the face of a man or a woman, and the body of an animal – such as a lion or a bull. These types of monsters were very common in Greek and Egyptian mythologies. The Egyptian sphinx was a combination of a man and a lion, while the Greek centaur had the torso of a man and the limbs and body of a horse. Most of these creatures were evil, but some were wise and even represented the gods.

The lamassu of Mesopotamia was similar to the sphinx

MAGICAL BEINGS

Most monsters and beasts had powers of magic, which they used for both good and evil purposes. The unicorn, for example, was able to cure diseases, while a basilisk could turn any living being into stone with a mere look. Magical beings that helped humans included Baku, the Japanese creature that ate nightmares, and Pegasus, the winged horse of the Greeks that helped many legendary heroes in their missions.

MIXED BAG

Imagine a monster with the wings and beak of an eagle, the body of a lion, the tail of a snake, and the ears of a horse! Monsters like the griffin were a prominent part of mythology. They were often a mixture of one or more animals or birds. Such monsters and beasts are to be found in most European mythologies. Even the dragons of the Chinese were a combination of many animals such as frog, snake, tiger, eagle and fish.

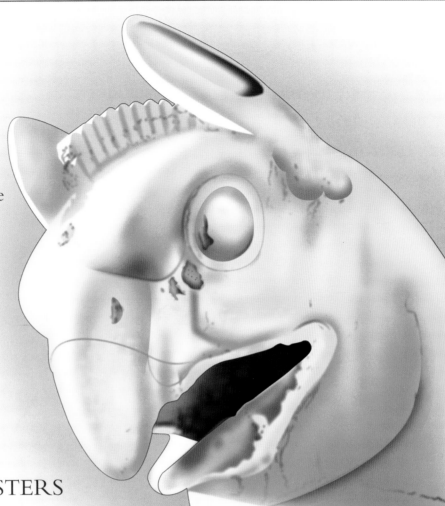

HIDDEN MONSTERS

Most monsters and beasts are the creation of the human mind, yet it is possible that some of these imaginary creatures are connected to similar animals of the past. Many experts believe that some mythological creatures could have existed. Such creatures are called cryptids and the study of these beasts is known as cryptozoology. The word 'crypto' comes from the Greek term *kryptos*, meaning 'hidden'. One of the best-known examples of such monsters is the giant squid. Scientists believe that this gigantic creature may in fact have started the tales of the Scandinavian monster, the Kraken.

Like an eagle, the griffin was thought to build nests, but instead of eggs it laid agates. It was believed that the female griffin laid the agates in a huge cave with a narrow entrance, and stood guard over them. When one of the griffins died, the other one spent the rest of its life alone. The griffin was also thought to guard gold mines and hidden treasures, much like the dragon. It was said that the griffin would pounce on people who came in search of gold or precious stones, and tear them to pieces.

MYTHS AND LEGENDS

A myth represents the beliefs and traditions of a particular culture. It contains religious and magical explanations for events. Myths try to answer questions about how the Earth was born, and the role of the gods in creating the Universe. Legends, on the other hand, talk about historical events. They could be partially or even fully true. The adventures of Robin Hood and King Arthur are legends, while the stories about the Greek gods are myths.

MONSTERS OF EGYPT

The myths and legends of ancient Egyptians span over a period of almost three thousand years. Apart from their legion of gods and goddesses, the ancient Egyptians also believed in evil forces. Egyptian mythology is full of stories about the battle between good and evil. It also contains stories of strange mythical beasts like Apep and the phoenix.

THE MONSTER OF NUN

Apep, also known as Apophis, was a huge snake that lived in Nun, the endless ocean. Each night it attacked Re's boat as it sailed through the underworld. It was believed that Apep was a Sun god, before Re took over. This was the reason for Apep's hatred of Re. The battle between the gods and Apep often caused stormy weather. At times Apep even swallowed the boat causing solar eclipses, but its success was short-lived. Apep was killed several times by Re's guardian, but always came back to life and continued his attacks.

HOLY BULLS

Bulls held a very important position in Egyptian mythology. Black bulls with a white triangle on the forehead were considered to represent Apis, the holy bull. Apis was believed to be the *ka*, or life force, of Ptah, a creator god. Apis was also thought to be a symbol of the pharaoh. Bulls that represented Apis were kept in the temple, and the future was predicted by studying their movements. When these bulls were 25 years old, they were killed and buried with much ceremony.

A book titled The Book of Overthrowing Apep *contains spells for defeating Apep. These spells were read out every day by ancient priests in the temple of Ra in Thebes*

PHOENIX

The phoenix was a mythical Sunbird associated with Re, the Sun god. Ancient Egyptians knew the bird as *benu*. The phoenix lived near a well. At dawn, it bathed in the well and sang a song so melodious that even Re stopped to listen. Every 500 or 1,461 years, the bird built a nest and set it on fire. It then threw itself into the flames. A new phoenix rose from the flames. It enclosed the ashes of the old phoenix in an egg of myrrh and left it at Re's temple in Heliopolis. The phoenix thus symbolised life after death, and was also regarded as a representation of the resurrection of Osiris, the god of fertility as well as the ruler of the underworld.

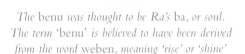

The benu *was thought to be Ra's* ba, *or soul. The term 'benu' is believed to have been derived from the word* weben, *meaning 'rise' or 'shine'*

EATER OF THE DEAD

Egyptian mythology contained stories about a creature called Ammut, or Ammit. It was often depicted as having a crocodile's head, and the upper body of a lion and the lower parts of a hippopotamus. Ammut lived in the Hall of Two Truths, where the soul of a dead person was usually taken. The heart of the dead was placed on the Scales of Justice and weighed against a feather of Ma'at, the goddess of truth, justice and order. If the heart weighed more than the feather, Ammut ate it up, destroying the soul forever.

The name Ammut means 'swallower of the dead'. Ammut was never worshipped as a goddess

MOTHER MONSTER

Monsters and beasts were an important part of Greek mythology. The mythical creatures of the ancient Greeks were terrifying and were considered the enemies of the gods. Most were the children of the chief monsters Echidna and Typhon.

A MONSTROUS COUPLE

Typhon was born to Gaia, the goddess personifying the Earth, while Echidna was born to Gaia's daughter, Ceto. Echidna was depicted as a serpent with the face of a woman. She married the hundred-headed Typhon and had several children with him. Both Echidna and Typhon were enemies of the gods. After a long battle, Zeus, the ruler of the gods, imprisoned Typhon under Mount Etna, but let Echidna and her children live.

In some legends, Heracles captured Cerberus with kindness, while in other versions he dragged the dog out of the Underworld

Many Greek scholars identified Typhon with Seth, the Egyptian god of chaos

THE HOUNDS OF ECHIDNA

Two of Echidna's children were dogs. One of them, Cerberus, was the watchdog of the Underworld, and had three heads and a snake for a tail. The two-headed Orthrus was responsible for guarding the cattle of Geryon, the winged giant. The mythical Greek hero Heracles, a son of Zeus, killed Orthrus during his attempt to steal Geryon's cattle and, as the last of his labours, dragged Cerburus to the surface.

 LADON AND HYDRA

Ladon and Hydra were also Echidna's
children. Ladon was a dragon
with a hundred heads. It
guarded the gardens of
the Hesperides, a group
of nymphs in Greek
mythology. Hydra
was a water monster
with nine heads and
poisonous breath. It lived in the lake of
Lerna and guarded the underwater entrance
to the Underworld. As a part of his 'twelve
labours', Heracles had to kill Hydra. Before
confronting the monster, Heracles covered his
mouth and nose to guard against its poisonous
breath. He then began to cut off the monster's
heads; but every time he cut a head, two new ones
grew in its place. Finally, Heracles turned to his
nephew Iolaus for help. As Heracles cut each head,
Iolaus burned the wound with a piece of flaming
wood to prevent a new head from growing.

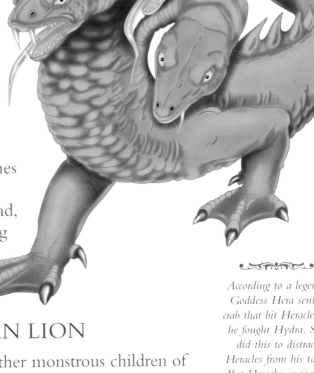

*According to a legend,
Goddess Hera sent a
crab that bit Heracles as
he fought Hydra. She
did this to distract
Heracles from his task.
But Heracles managed
to kill both the crab and
Hydra. After both her
beasts were killed, Hera
placed them among the
constellations in the sky*

CHIMERA AND THE NEMEAN LION

The Chimera and the Nemean Lion were the other monstrous children of
Echidna and Typhon. The Chimera was depicted as a creature with the head
of a lion, the body of a goat, and the tail of a dragon. The monster lived in
a place called Lycia, where it preyed on women, children and cattle. The
terrible creature was finally killed by the Greek hero Bellerophon with the
help of Pegasus, the winged horse. The Nemean Lion was a ferocious beast
that could not be harmed by any weapon. As the first of his 'twelve labours',
Heracles killed the lion by strangling it with his bare hands.

EAGLE OF MT CAUCASUS

Among Echidna's monstrous children was a gigantic
eagle named Ethon. When Prometheus, a Titan god,
stole fire from Mount Olympus and gave it to humans,
Zeus became angry. He punished Prometheus by having him
chained to Mount Caucasus, where Ethon fed on his liver. Every
night the liver healed and the eagle started all over again the next
day. It was left to Heracles to finally slay the eagle.

OTHER GREEK MONSTERS

Echidna was not the only one to give birth to monsters. Gaia, too, had monstrous children like Charybdis and Python. Beasts that were part human and part animal were also popular among ancient Greeks.

The ruins of the temple of Apollo at Delphi. It was believed that Apollo first came to Delphi in the form of a dolphin

PYTHON OF DELPHI

Python was a monstrous snake and the son of Gaia. It guarded the oracle of Delphi on Mount Parnassus. All those who lived near the mountain were scared of this snake as it destroyed crops and polluted the streams nearby with its poison. Finally, Apollo, the god of music and light, came to the rescue. Using his silver bow and golden arrows, Apollo killed the snake and had the oracle at Delphi dedicated to himself. He is said to have started the Pythian Games to commemorate the victory. The games comprised athletic and musical contests.

MONSTERS OF THE SEA

Charybdis and Scylla were a great danger to passing ships. Both used to be beautiful nymphs. Charybdis, the daughter of Poseidon, flooded lands to expand her father's underwater kingdom. Angry at her deeds, Zeus turned Charybdis into a water monster. Scylla was the daughter of Phorcys, a sea god. Glaucus, another sea god, fell in love with Scylla, but she did not return his love. Glaucus went to the sorceress Circe for a love potion. Circe herself fell in love with Glaucus; but he could not forget Scylla. An angry Circe then turned Scylla into a monster with twelve feet and six heads.

CENTAURS

Centaurs were creatures with the head and torso of a human, and the body of a horse. They lived on Mount Pelion in Thessaly and were known to kidnap young, unmarried women. Centaurs were believed to be the children of Ixion, king of Thessaly, and Nephele, a rain cloud. Most of them, except Pholus and Chiron, were wild and cruel. Chiron was a wise and kind centaur who knew the art of healing. Heracles accidentally wounded Chiron with a poisoned arrow. Chiron died after he gave up his immortality to escape the unbearable pain.

Once, the centaurs tried to kidnap Hippodamia, on the day of her wedding to Pirithous, the king of the Lapiths. A bloody battle ensued, in which the centaurs were defeated

Ariadne, the fertility goddess, gave Theseus a spool of thread that he unwound as he went into the Labyrinth in search of the Minotaur. The thread helped Theseus to find his way out of the maze after accomplishing his task

THE CURSE OF CRETE

Before Minos became the king of Crete, he made a request to Poseidon that he send him a white bull as a sign that the gods approved of his rule. He promised to later sacrifice the same bull to honour the gods. Poseidon sent Minos a beautiful white bull. Minos was so impressed by it that he forgot his promise and sacrificed another bull, instead. When Poseidon realised what had happened, he became angry and made Pasipha, the wife of Minos, have a child with the white bull. This was the Minotaur, a creature with a bull's head and tail, and a man's body. Minos locked up the hideous monster in a huge maze called the Labyrinth. Every ninth year, young men and women were sent to the Labyrinth as food for the beast, which was finally killed by the Greek hero Theseus.

THE SPHINX

The sphinx was one of the most popular creatures in mythology. Both ancient Egyptians and Greeks believed in this mythical beast, but the sphinx of each culture was very different. For the Egyptians, the sphinx was a creature worthy of respect; while the sphinx of the ancient Greeks was a terrible monster that killed people.

 THE EGYPTIAN SPHINX

In ancient Egypt the sphinx was a creature with a lion's body and a man's head. The people there believed in different kinds of sphinxes. The criosphinx had a ram's head, while the hierocosphinx had the head of a hawk. The sphinx with the human head was known as the androsphinx. Sphinxes were seen as protectors and their statues adorned temple entrances. The Great Sphinx was regarded as a representation of Hor-em-Akht ('Horus in the Horizon'). Hor-em-Akht was actually Horus, the god of the pharaohs, and in this form he was depicted as the Sun god.

Horus was often represented by a falcon or a hawk wearing the crowns of Upper and Lower Egypt

THE GREEK SPHINX

The Greek sphinx was born to Echidna and Typhon. It was a cruel monster symbolising destruction and bad fortune. The creature had a lion's body and a woman's head. It also had the wings of an eagle. In Greek mythology, the goddess Hera sent the sphinx from its mountain abode to trouble the people of Thebes. The creature sat on a rock at the entrance of the city asking all passersby a strange riddle. She strangled all those who could not answer it. Soon, nobody dared to go in and out of the city.

THE SPHINX MEETS HER MATCH

The people of Thebes announced that anyone who could answer the riddle would be rewarded with the throne of Thebes as well as the queen's hand in marriage. When a brave young stranger named Oedipus heard about the problems of Thebes, he decided to try his luck. He approached the sphinx. The riddle was: "What creature has one voice and walks on four legs in the morning, two legs in the afternoon, and three in the evening?" Oedipus replied, "Man. As a child, he crawls on his hands and feet, as a young man he walks on two legs, and in old age he uses a cane." Now that the riddle was solved, the distressed sphinx threw herself from the rock and died.

Oedipus answered the riddle of the sphinx. After getting rid of the sphinx, Oedipus married the queen of Thebes

The Great Sphinx at Giza is thought to represent Harmakhis, or 'Horus in the Horizon.' In this form, Horus was associated with the rising Sun

THE SPHINX AT GIZA

The Great Sphinx was built by the Egyptian pharaoh Khafre. Over the years, all except the head of the statue got buried in sand. Once, an Egyptian prince named Thutmosis came upon the sphinx. The tired prince decided to rest under it. While he slept, Thutmosis had a dream in which the sphinx told him that he would become the pharaoh if he freed it from the sand. The prince did as he was told and was rewarded with the crown of Egypt.

MESOPOTAMIAN MONSTERS

The mythologies of the ancient Sumerians, Akkadians, Assyrians and Babylonians had many mythical beasts, both good and evil. The monsters of the Mesopotamians, as in many cultures, were opposed to the gods. The most popular battle of these was the one between the Babylonian god Marduk and Tiamat, the giant serpent.

ZU AND THE TABLETS OF DESTINY

Zu, also called Anzu, was a giant bird that could breathe fire and water. This part-man and part-bird creature represented thunderclouds, and was very powerful. Enlil, one of the main gods of the Mesopotamians, appointed Zu as the guardian of his bath chamber. One day, while Enlil was bathing, Zu stole the Tablets of Destiny that gave the god power to control the universe. Zu hid the tablets on a mountain. When Enlil found out, he approached Anu, the king of gods. Anu sent an army of gods to retrieve the tablets. In one story Marduk killed the storm bird, while according to another legend, Ninurta the war god killed it.

Some considered Zu to be a lesser god and the son of Siris, the bird goddess. Zu was often depicted as an eagle with a lion's head

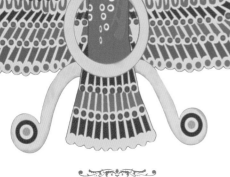

The Pazuzu was often depicted with the body of a man and the tail of a scorpion

 ## WINGED BEASTS

Ancient Mesopotamians believed in several winged beasts. The Pazuzu was the most feared among these. It was hideous to look at, with its lion's claws and scorpion's tail. This winged beast represented the southeast storm wind. It lived in the desert and was believed to be the cause of all diseases. Another well-known winged beast in Mesopotamian mythology was the lamassu. This winged lion had the head of a man – making it similar to the sphinx in Egyptian and Greek mythologies. Like the Egyptian sphinx, the lamassu was seen as a protective spirit and kept at the entrances of temples and palaces.

 ## TIAMAT'S REVENGE

Ancient Mesopotamians believed that Tiamat was a female serpent who represented the endless ocean. Tiamat and her husband Apsu, the personification of freshwater, were the creators of all beings including the gods. In the Babylonian epic *Enuma elish*, Tiamat and Apsu grew annoyed with their noisy children and decided to kill them. When the gods discovered the couple's plans, they killed Apsu. Tiamat was so angry that she created an army of monsters to destroy the gods. Marduk, upon gaining the promise of the other gods that he would be recognised as their supreme, killed Tiamat in battle and created the Earth and the sky with her body.

The death of his dear friend Enkidu prompted Gilgamesh to set out in search of eternal life

BULL OF HEAVEN

The Bull of Heaven, which represented drought, made its appearance in the famous Babylonian book, *Epic of Gilgamesh*. This epic told the story of Gilgamesh, a Babylonian king. Ishtar, the goddess of love, tried to woo Gilgamesh, but did not succeed. Gilgamesh knew about Ishtar's other lovers whom she either killed or mutilated in rage. The angry Ishtar went to her father Anu for help. The king of gods sent the Bull of Heaven to destroy Gilgamesh, but the king managed to slay the bull with the help of his friend Enkidu. He then sent the headless body of the bull to Ishtar. The gods, to avenge the killing of the bull, struck Enkidu with a disease that killed him.

DRAGONS OF EUROPE

The dragon is probably among the most popular of mythical creatures. Dragon tales are a prominent part of mythologies across the world. They are found in almost all cultures including Chinese, Japanese, Indian and European, but they look quite different in each.

In Greek mythology, Goddess Hera put Draco, the dragon, in charge of guarding the golden apples of the Hesperides. Draco was killed by the Greek hero Heracles who, as part of his 'labours', had to obtain the golden apples. Goddess Hera rewarded her favourite servant by turning him into a constellation

A DRAGON'S LIFE

In European mythology, a dragon is usually shown as a huge serpent–like creature. Some European dragons are winged, while others like the wyrm do not have wings. Almost all European dragons have four legs. The exceptions include the wyrm, which has no legs, and the wyvern, which has only two legs. Again, nearly all the European dragons breathe fire. Some even spit out poisonous gases. In European mythology, the dragon was depicted as an evil creature that preferred to live alone. It usually lived in caves beneath waterfalls or near lakes.

 WYVERNS

The wyvern is much smaller than the dragon and has two hind legs with talons similar to those of an eagle. It has bat-like wings and does not breathe fire, although some were believed to do so. A distinct feature of the wyvern is its long, barbed tail. Other creatures similar to the wyvern include the lindworm and the sea-wyvern. The lindworm usually lacks legs and wings, although some were believed to have two legs. Lindworms mostly fed on cattle. They were also said to enter church cemeteries and dig up dead bodies. The sea-wyvern was different from the wyvern only in having the tail of a fish.

Wyverns became popular during the Middle Ages, when they were thought to help sorcerers with spells

BASILISK

Roman mythology talked about a dragon-like creature called a basilisk, or cockatrice. It was believed to have been born from a rooster egg hatched by a toad. There were two kinds of basilisk. One of them burned everything that came near, while the other destroyed all living things with just a look. The only way to destroy a basilisk was to hold a mirror in front of it so that it would turn itself into stone. It was also said that the basilisk died immediately if it heard a rooster crow.

The basilisk was believed to have had many powers. It was said that the monster could turn a living thing into stone with a look or even the sound of its voice!

WHAT'S IN A NAME?

The word 'dragon' comes from the Latin *draco*, which in turn was derived from the Greek *drakon*, meaning 'that which sees,' referring to the dragon's excellent eyesight. In Scandinavian mythology the dragon was called *wurm*, while in Old English it was *wyrm*, meaning 'snake'. Some people also believed that the word 'dragon' has its origins in the Old Norse term *draugr* – it was used to describe a spirit that guarded the burial mound of a king.

DRAGOns OF BRiTAin

Dragon legends were a major part of British culture at one time. Most dragon tales in Britain had their roots in Celtic or Norse mythology. In the past, people identified shooting stars and other strange lights in the sky with dragons. Dragons were considered to be a bad omen in Britain, as in all other European cultures.

John Lambton wore an armour with spikes, so that when the worm tried to coil itself around him, the spikes cut through its body

 WORM

The most common form of dragon in British legends was the worm. This creature was believed to look like a gigantic snake. It had huge fangs and poisonous breath. It was wingless and had no legs. The worm was capable of joining together even after being cut into pieces. By the Middle Ages, dragons began to be associated with the devil. People who killed dragons were conferred with sainthood. A popular legend is that of St George, a brave knight who killed a dragon to rescue a princess.

THE LAMBTON WORM

Young John Lambton, heir to Lambton Hall, once caught an eel-like creature while fishing, and threw it into an old well nearby. Years passed and the worm grew huge and began to terrorise the village. Finally, John killed the beast with the help of a local witch. Before he set off on his mission, the witch told John that after killing the worm he would have to kill the first living being that crossed his path. John, however, could not keep his promise, as the first living being he met afterwards was his father. Thereafter a curse befell the family, and nine generations of Lambtons died tragically.

MERLIN AND THE WELSH DRAGON

Vortigern, a Celtic chieftain, ruled Britain during the Anglo-Saxon invasion. Following the attack, Vortigern was forced to flee to Wales. There, in Snowdon, the king decided to build a fort, but the walls kept falling down. The king's advisors told him that a fatherless child would have to be sacrificed to please the bad spirit that lived there. After a long search the king's men came upon Merlin, who did not have a father. Merlin told the king about two dragons, one red and the other white, who lived under the hill. Merlin said that the red dragon represented the Welsh, while the white stood for the Anglo-Saxons, and it was their fights that caused the walls to fall. Thus, it was only after the dragons were released that the fort could finally be built.

The legendary red dragon can be seen on the present Welsh flag

NESSIE

The Loch Ness monster is the most popular of all British legends about monsters. Fondly known as Nessie, it is believed to live in Loch Ness, near Inverness in Scotland. Most people who claimed to have seen the monster describe a gigantic lizard-like creature with two humps and a tail. The first known reference to Nessie was made in the biography of St Columba, an Irish monk who helped establish Christianity in Scotland. It is related that St Columba was on his way to meet a Scottish chieftain when he saw a huge beast about to attack a swimmer. The priest called out God's name and told the beast to go back. The beast did so and the swimmer was saved!

DRAGONS OF THE NORSE PEOPLE

Norse mythology is filled with dragon stories. The dragons of the Norse people were called wyrms. It was these wyrms that gave rise to the worm of Britain. Some of the well-known Norse dragons include the Jörmungand, Nidhogg and Fafnir, the dwarf who turned into a dragon.

THE MIDGARD SERPENT

Jörmungand, also known as the Midgard Serpent, was one of the three monstrous children of Loki, the trickster god, and his wife, Angrboda. Jörmungand grew so big that the gods were scared it would destroy the world. Therefore, Odin threw the wyrm into the sea. Nevertheless, Jörmungand kept growing until it surrounded the Earth, biting its own tail.

Fafnir took the form of a dragon to drive his brother away, so that he could keep all the gold for himself. Ever since, the dragon has been used as a symbol for greed by the Norse people

ARCH RIVALS

In Norse mythology, Thor the thunder god was Jörmungand's biggest enemy. There were many instances when the two confronted each other. In one such encounter, Thor came upon the wyrm disguised as a giant cat. Utgard-Loki, the king of the frost giants, once asked Thor to prove his strength. As part of his test, Thor was asked to lift the giant cat. Thor did not realise that the cat was actually Jörmungand and could not lift it. It was believed that in Ragnarök, the final battle, Thor would kill Jörmungand but be able to walk only nine steps before dying from the wyrm's poison.

EATER OF THE DEAD

Nidhogg was a huge serpent that continuously chewed at the roots of the World Tree, Yggdrasil. The creature's name meant 'eater of corpses', and true to its name, Nidhogg ate dead bodies to survive. The beast constantly fought with the eagle that lived on top of the tree. Nidhogg was not the only creature that attacked the Yggdrasil. Other serpents like Graback, Grafvolluth, Goin and Moin also gnawed at the roots of the World Tree.

FOR THE LOVE OF GOLD

One of the most popular dragon tales in Norse mythology is that of the dwarf Fafnir, who turned into a dragon. Fafnir was the son of Hreidmar, the dwarf king. He had two brothers, Regin and Otr. When Loki accidentally killed Otr, the gods gave Hreidmar a magical ring called Andvarinaut and some gold as a peace offering. The Andvarinaut and the gold had previously been stolen by Loki from another dwarf, Andvari. When Loki stole the ring, Andvari cursed it. When this cursed ring now came into Hreidmar's possession, his sons Fafnir and Regin killed him for it. Fafnir then took on the form of a dragon and drove Regin away. Later, Regin sent his foster son, Sigurd, to get the gold and the ring. Sigurd killed Fafnir and took the gold. When he realised that Regin would kill him for the gold, Sigurd killed Regin too.

Andvari the dwarf had the power to change himself into a fish whenever he wanted to. It was when Andvari was swimming in the river as a fish that Loki caught him with a net. He then refused to let Andvari go unless the latter gave up the Andvarinaut, a magical ring that helped Andvari to become rich

OTHER NORSE MONSTERS

Dragons are not the only beasts that can be found in Norse mythology. The Norse people believe in many other monsters like Fenrir and Garm. Most of them were the children of Loki, the trickster god, and Angrboda, a giantess.

FENRIR

The eldest child of Loki and Angrboda was a gigantic wolf named Fenrir. It was predicted that Fenrir would destroy the world, so the gods locked him up in a cage. Soon Fenrir began to grow. When the gods saw how enormous the wolf had become, they decided to chain him up, but Fenrir broke even the strongest chain. The gods finally decided to tie him up with a magic chain. It was believed that on the Ragnarök, Fenrir would break his chains to take part in the battle against the gods. He would kill Odin and in turn would be killed by Odin's son, Vidar.

The silken rope that binds Fenrir is called gleipnir. It was made by the dwarfs on Odin's request. The gleipnir is made of the sound of a cat's footfall, the beard of a woman, the tendons of a bear, the breath of a fish, mountain roots and a bird's spittle

GARM

Like Cerberus in Greek mythology, Garm guarded the entrance to Helheim, the Norse underworld. The hound lived in a cave called Gnipa. It had four eyes and was covered in blood. Only those who gave alms to the poor could hope to win Garm's trust with Hel cake. It was believed that Garm would howl to signal the beginning of the Ragnarök. The dog would join the giants in their battle against the gods. During the battle, Garm and Tyr, the god of war, would kill each other.

It is believed that Garm would howl three times before the Ragnarök. The first howl would bring in the Fimbulwinter, or three successive winters during which there will be several wars. The second howl would be followed by the attack of the giants, and the last howl predicts a new and better world

KRAKEN

Norwegian and Icelandic sailors of the past believed in an enormous monster known to them as the Kraken. This sea monster was believed to be half octopus and half crab. The Kraken was said to drag down even the largest ships and feed on the helpless sailors. As the creature went back into the water, it created a huge whirlpool that could suck everything nearby into its depths. The whirlpool was so powerful, its swirling currents could suck in huge vessels too.

GODLY BEASTS

Not all beasts in Norse mythology were evil. Some of them were associated with the gods. These divine beasts included Odin's ravens and Thor's magical goats. Huginn and Muninn were the two ravens of Odin, the king of gods. Huginn stood for 'thought' and Muninn meant 'memory'. Every day these ravens flew across the Earth and gathered information for Odin. They returned to their master at night and told him about all that they heard and saw. The chariot of Thor, the god of thunder, was drawn by two magical goats – Tanngrisnir, or tooth-grinder, and Tanngnjóstr, or tooth-gnasher. The god also used to eat these goats, though he would later place the bones and skin together and return them to life with his hammer.

DRAGOПS OF THE EAST

Dragons were a very important part of the mythologies of various Asian countries, especially China, Korea and Japan. They represented wisdom and strength, and were sources of good luck. The body of the Eastern dragon was usually made of various other animals. The dragon was believed to have the body of a snake, belly of a frog, head of a camel, eyes of a hare, paws of a tiger, claws of an eagle, and scales of a carp.

A MAGICAL MONSTER

The Eastern dragon was completely different from the Western one. The biggest difference was that most Eastern dragons were considered to be good and helpful, unlike their evil cousins in the West. They did not have wings like the Western dragons. Instead, Eastern dragons used magic to help them fly. The dragons of the East were associated with water. They were said to be responsible for a good rainfall and rich harvest. The Eastern dragons were also believed to ward off evil. In China, the five-clawed dragon was a symbol of the monarchy.

The dragon is a major part of Chinese culture and tradition. In fact, no Chinese New Year procession is complete without the dragon dance. In this, a team of dancers carry a huge cloth dragon on poles and dance along the streets

A TALE OF TOES

The dragons of China, Korea and Japan were quite different from each other. One of the most interesting differences was in the number of toes. The Chinese Imperial dragon had five toes; in comparison, the common Chinese dragons had only four. The Chinese believed that dragons originated in China. As they travelled further away from their native land, these dragons lost their toes. When they reached Korea they had only four, and by the time they were in Japan the toes reduced to three. If the dragons travelled any further, they lost all toes and could no longer walk. The Japanese, for their part, believed that dragons originated in Japan and that they grew toes as they flew away from their country.

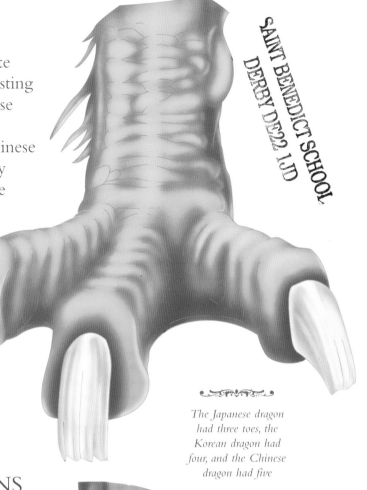

SAINT BENEDICT SCHOOL
DERBY DE22 1JD

The Japanese dragon had three toes, the Korean dragon had four, and the Chinese dragon had five

MALE AND FEMALE DRAGONS

Eastern dragons could be male or female. There were many physical differences that helped to distinguish the two. Male dragons were usually depicted as holding clubs in their tails, while the females held fans. The male dragons had horns that were thinner towards the base of the head, and bigger and stronger towards the front. Females had manes that were neat and shapely, while the manes of the male dragons were untidy and rigid. The females were smaller in size and had thinner scales. The males had stouter bodies.

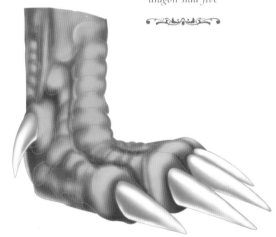

PEARLS OF WISDOM

The Eastern dragon was known for its magical pearls that brought luck. Some people believed that these pearls were made from the dragon's spit. The pearls were also thought to be the teardrops of the Moon. As these tears fell, some were swallowed by oysters, while others were caught by dragons. Not all dragons owned pearls, and the ones that had a pearl guarded the precious stone with their lives.

THE ORIENTAL DRAGON

The Chinese, or Oriental, dragon is the best known among the Eastern dragons. The Chinese associated their dragons with weather and water. The dragon is also an important animal in the Chinese zodiac. The ancient Chinese also thought that the dragon represented their emperors.

THE MAGIC OF NINE

The Chinese considered the number nine to be auspicious, so it is only natural that they connected the dragon with this number. A Chinese dragon was believed to have 117 scales – 81 representing good and 36 for evil. All these numbers are multiples of nine. The Chinese also believed that the dragon had nine children. Among them were bixi, resembling a giant land turtle; the beastly-looking chiwen; pulao, which looked like a small dragon; and bi'an, which looked more like a tiger.

THE NINE DRAGONS

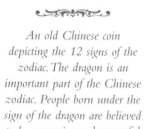
An old Chinese coin depicting the 12 signs of the zodiac. The dragon is an important part of the Chinese zodiac. People born under the sign of the dragon are believed to be aggressive and successful

In Chinese mythology, there are nine types of dragons. The first group, called Tianlong, were celestial dragons that pulled the chariots of gods and guarded their homes. Shenlong, the spiritual dragons, controlled the wind and rain, while Fucanglong were underworld dragons that guarded buried treasures. Dilong, the Earth dragons, managed the rivers and streams. Yinglong was a winged dragon that served Huangdi, the Yellow Emperor. Panlong were water dragons and Qiulong had horns. Huanglong, the 'yellow' dragon, was believed to have taught writing to the legendary Chinese Emperor Fu Shi. Additionally, there were the four Dragon Kings that ruled the four seas. They lived in crystal palaces guarded by shrimps and crabs. These dragons could also take on the form of humans.

DRAGON IN THE MAKING

The Chinese believed that each dragon went through various stages in its lifetime. It spent the first five hundred years or so as a water snake. The next stage was as a scaled creature, *chiao*, and this lasted for another 500 years approximately. Then the dragon grew into a hornless *lung*. The *lung* soon grew horns, gaining a wiser appearance in the process. If a dragon lived for more than 2,000 years, it gained wings.

The various stages in a dragon's life, from a water snake to the 2,000-year old winged dragon

DRAGON'S GATE

The Chinese believed that just as dragons could take on the form of animals, so could various animals turn into dragons. One of the most popular legends is associated with the Dragon's Gate. It was believed that Yu, a golden dragon that was also a rain god, created the rivers of China by dragging his tail trough the soil. As he made the Yellow River, Yu came across some cliffs. Yu made a hole in the cliffs so that the river could flow through. He named it the Dragon's Gate. It is said that if a fish swam against the current and leapt through the Dragon's Gate, it would become a dragon.

NAGAS OF INDIA

Hindu mythology is one of the most varied and colourful. The people of India believe in thousands of gods and goddesses. They also believe in a similar number of monsters and beasts. A popular legendary creature in Hindu mythology is the naga. The word 'naga' means 'snake' in Sanskrit. The female counterpart of a naga is called a nagini.

GUARDIANS OF RAIN

Nagas are the closest Indian relatives of the Chinese dragon, but they cannot be entirely considered as dragons. They are depicted as either snakes, or part human and part snake. They are believed to live in Patala-loka, the Hindu underworld. The nagas have many similarities to the Chinese dragon. Like the Chinese, the Indians associate the nagas with rain. If they are unhappy with humans, they also cause floods and drought. Nagas are worshipped even today, especially in the southern parts of India.

Mucalinda protecting Lord Buddha from the storm

FAMOUS NAGAS

The most recognised of all nagas were Ananta, Vasuki, Mucalinda and Manasa. Ananta is a thousand-headed naga whose huge coiled body floats on the endless ocean as a bed on which Lord Vishnu rests. Manasa is a *nagini*, who is said to provide protection against snakebites. Mucalinda is known as the naga who protected Lord Buddha from a storm as he meditated under the Bodhi tree. It is believed that Mucalinda came up from his palace in the underworld and protected Buddha with his hood. When the storm cleared, the snake bowed before the lord and returned to his kingdom.

THE KING OF NAGAS

Vasuki is the king of nagas. It is said that both *deva*s, or the lesser gods, and *asura*s, or demons, churned the cosmic 'ocean of milk' to gain *amrita*, the nectar of immortality. Vasuki was used as a rope for the churning and he threw up poison. Fearing that the poison would destroy the world, the god Shiva swallowed it. Seeing this, Shiva's wife Parvati held his neck to stop the poison from spreading through his body. This made Shiva's face and neck turn blue, earning him the name Neelakantha, meaning 'one with the blue neck.'

NAGAS OF THE WORLD

People of Thailand, Malay, Java and Cambodia also believe in nagas. In Thailand and Java, the naga is a rich god who lives in the underworld. In Malay, nagas are dragons with many heads. The nagas of Cambodia lived in the Pacific Ocean and owned a huge kingdom. The naga king's daughter was believed to have married the king of ancient Cambodia and created the Cambodians.

Statue of Garuda at Angkor Wat, Cambodia. Garuda is considered to be the biggest enemy of the nagas and is often depicted as holding a naga in his talons

THE ELIXIR OF LIFE

In Hindu mythology, the divine eagle Garuda once stole *amrita* from heaven. Indra, the king of *deva*s, managed to get it back. Just as he was returning with the nectar, though, a few drops fell on the ground. It is said that the nagas slithered over it. Ever since, snakes are able to shed their old skin and grow a new one.

PERSIAN MONSTERS

The mythologies of Persia (present-day Iran) and Arabia had many monsters and beasts. They related tales of gigantic birds, dragons and chimera – creatures formed of different animals.

AZHI DAHAKA

The Persians believed in a giant serpent called Azhi Dahaka, or the 'great snake.' Azhi Dahaka was often considered a dragon that served Angra Mainyu, the god of evil. The 'great snake' was depicted as a three-headed monster with six eyes and a thousand senses. He stole cattle and fed on snakes, scorpions and other poisonous creatures. He also caused storms and diseases. The snake was captured by the Persian hero Thraetaona. Since the monster could not be killed, Thraetaona chained him to a volcano instead. It was believed that Azhi Dahaka would break free during the final battle between the good and the evil forces. It would cause heavy destruction before finally drowning in Ayohsust, the river of fire.

A WISE OLD BIRD

Persian mythology talked about a gigantic bird called the Simurgh. This winged monster was depicted in the likeness of a peacock, with the head of a dog and the claws of a lion. The bird was so huge that it could carry elephants and camels. It usually lived in places with plenty of water. It was told that the bird was so old that it had seen the world destroyed three times, and for the same reason was thought to be very wise.

Sometimes the Simurgh was depicted with a human face. This gigantic bird lived in a nest on the 'Tree of Knowledge'

AN ELEPHANT'S NIGHTMARE

The Roc, or Rukh, and the Simurgh were very similar creatures. Like the Simurgh, the Roc was a gigantic bird that fed on elephants. The Roc became more popular because of its appearance in the tales of Sinbad the Sailor. The enormous white bird had feathers the size of palm leaves. In one of the adventures of Sinbad, the brave sailor was stranded on a deserted island. He had landed on the island with his merchant friends. While his friends were busy collecting fruits and flowers, Sinbad fell asleep. When he woke up, he found the ship had gone, leaving him behind. As he looked around, he came across an enormous egg. The egg was that of the Roc. Sinbad quickly hid behind the egg and waited for the bird. When the bird returned to its nest, Sinbad tied himself to one of its legs. The next day, the bird flew off in search of prey, unaware that Sinbad was enjoying a free ride on its leg!

Sinbad clinging on to the feet of the Roc

PERSIAN CHIMERA

The manticore was a kind of chimera with a man's head, a lion's body, and a scorpion's tail. The manticore's tail could shoot out poisonous spines to injure its prey. Sometimes the monster was depicted as having wings. The beast was a man-eater. It was said that it killed its victim with the poisonous darts from its tail. The creature then ate the person completely, not even sparing the bones! Thus it came about that whenever somebody disappeared, the people attributed it to the manticore.

DRAGONS OF THE AMERICAS

The 'dragons' of the Americas did not really fit the usual description of the creature. These beasts were more snake-like, with no legs or wings. Yet, they were different from the snakes that we see around us. These mythical American snakes had feathers and magical powers. They were also associated with rain and fertility, like the Eastern dragons, and were even considered to be gods.

FEATHERED SERPENT

American mythology gave much importance to the feathered serpent. Quetzalcóatl, one of the main gods of the ancient Americans, was depicted as a feathered serpent. The feathered serpents were reputed to be wise and aware of all the secrets in the world. However, they were believed to be timid creatures that hid from people. These beasts resembled an enormous snake, with bright blue and green feathers. They also had a crown of feathers on the head and wattles under the chin. The body parts were said to possess magical properties. If a person drank the serpent's blood, he could talk in the serpent's language. The serpent's eyes, dried and mixed with honey, could cure headaches; and its tooth, planted in the ground, could become a soldier ready to fight!

The carved head of a feathered serpent on the Temple of Quetzalcóatl in Teotihuacan, Mexico. It was believed that the gods gathered in this city to discuss the creation of man

HORNED SERPENT

The feathered serpent lived on land, while the horned serpent lived under water. It was the biggest enemy of the divine thunderbird. The most noticeable feature of this beast was its horns – one red in colour and the other green. The horned serpents swam in deep waters, with their mouths open and ready to grab anything that came their way. These creatures were wingless, but had both gills and lungs to help them breathe on land and under water. The heart of the horned serpent was unique. It kept on beating even after the creature died.

THE PIASA

The 'bird that devours men,' as the Piasa is known, closely resembled the dragon. It had a human face with a lizard-like body, four bird-like legs, and a pair of huge leathery wings. It also had the horns of a stag and the beard of a tiger. It was believed that the Piasa inhabited the cliffs and was not always a man-eater. It used to consume large mammals, deer being a particular favourite. One day a fight started between two tribes who lived in the area, and many people were killed. The Piasa fed on the dead bodies, thereby developing a taste for human flesh. Finally, it was a brave warrior named Masatonga who succeeded in killing the dreaded monster.

The Piasa was finally killed by a Native American chief. The chief lured the beast out of its hiding place and his men, who were hiding behind trees, killed the Piasa with poisoned arrows

MONSTER BY THE LAKE

Native Americans believed in a lake monster called Amhuluk, said to have lived in the lakes of Oregon. It was depicted as a large snake with horns, and was known to drown people. One legend relates how Amhuluk once captured two children with its horns and carried them to the lake. The grief-stricken father went to the lake to see his children. For five days the children came to him, but after that they disappeared forever.

NATIVE AMERICAN MONSTERS

Animals and birds play an important role in the mythologies of the North and South Americas. Even the gods of these regions are part animal or bird. The Native Americans especially have a huge collection of tales regarding strange animals. Some of these beasts were considered helpful to humans, while others were completely evil in nature.

THIRSTY FOR BLOOD

A dreaded creature called the chupacabra was believed to exist in many parts of North America, especially Mexico. This creature was thought to drink the blood of farm animals, particularly goats, and hence the name 'goat sucker'. The tales of chupacabra attacks spread as more and more people began to lose their livestock. Most of the victims had two tiny holes in their necks. The creature was thought to hypnotise its prey and then suck its blood slowly. This gave rise to the legend of the chupacabra – a small, green bloodthirsty creature. Sometimes the monster was depicted as a lizard-like animal with greenish skin and sharp spines on its back. It was said to have the face of a dog, a forked tongue and large fangs. The creature hopped like a kangaroo. Other accounts described the chupacabra as a hairless wild dog.

THUNDERBIRD

The Native Americans believed in a powerful bird spirit they called the 'thunderbird'. It was said that lightning flashed from its eyes and that the flapping of its wings caused thunder. It was often depicted as having a second head on the lower part of its body. For the Native Americans, the thunderbird was the most important animal spirit in their culture. The thunderbird was considered to be helpful to humans, but the giant bird did not show any mercy while punishing evildoers. It was wise and kind, and even taught humans how to farm and build houses.

The physical description of the chupacabra varies from place to place. The most common description is that of a lizard-like beast with spines running down its back

WENDIGO

In Native American mythology, the wendigo was an animal spirit. It was known as the 'Spirit of Lonely Places' and was feared by all those who went into woods and other deserted places. The wendigo was believed to be half man and half beast, eating anything that came across its path – including humans. It had a heart of ice and possessed the power to change into any animal. The creature stayed away from sight and followed the lonely traveller, waiting for the right opportunity, and then pounced on the person. Once bitten by the monster, the victim too is believed to change into a wendigo.

A squonk in the process of dissolving itself in a pool of tears

TEARS OF SORROW

In the hemlock forests of northern Pennsylvania lived a peculiar beast called the squonk. This creature was extremely strange. Its skin was covered with so many warts that the squonk spent most of its time in hiding. One could hear the beast cry its heart out over it hideous appearance. Hunters who tried to catch the squonk realised that the creature often dissolved itself in a pool of tears. Once, a man managed to capture a squonk. He put it in a bag and started home. As he walked, he suddenly realised that the bag had become light. When he opened the bag he was stunned to see that there was nothing in it except liquid!

ABORIGINAL TALES

The Aborigines of Australia had many stories about their monsters and beasts. Giant snakes, fierce koalas, blood-sucking creatures and other strange-looking beasts formed an important part of the Aboriginal mythology.

 ## THE RAINBOW SNAKE

There were many different myths about the rainbow snake, but all believed that it was responsible for the creation of the Earth. The giant snake had a colourful skin and lived in lakes and pools. It is said that the snake formed gullies and deep channels for rivers as it slithered over the ground. Some tribes believed that the snake hid all the plants and waters of the Earth inside him. When they could not bear their hunger anymore, the people approached a priest for help. The priest turned himself into a kookaburra and distracted the snake, while the rest of the people cut open its body and released the plants and waters.

BUNYIP

In Aboriginal mythology, a bunyip was a terrible beast that lived in swamps, lakes, riverbeds and waterholes. The descriptions of the bunyip varied according to the tribe, but most of them attributed to the beast the tail of a horse, the tusks of a walrus, and flippers. The bunyip was said to feed on any animal or human that approached its living places. Horrible, spine-chilling cries could be heard when a bunyip attacked. This creature was also thought to cause diseases.

Stories about the rainbow snake varied among tribes, but all of them believed that the rainbow snake was the protector of man and that he also punished sinners

SAINT BENEDICT SCHOOL
DERBY DE22 1JD

DROP BEAR

The drop bear is another well-known creature from Aboriginal mythology. These beasts were believed to look like koalas, but were not as shy or timid. Drop bears ate meat and usually waited patiently on treetops for prey to come along. The beast then dropped on to the heads of the prey and quickly devoured it.

YARA-MA-YHA-WHO

The yara-ma-yha-who was half man and half beast. It was depicted as a furry little red man with a huge head and mouth. It had no teeth and swallowed its food whole. It sucked the victim's blood using its fingers and toes, which resembled the suckers of an octopus. Finally it swallowed the prey, only to regurgitate it after a nap. The prey at this point would still be alive! Hence, the Aborigines thought it better for a victim to be swallowed by the creature. That way, the chances of being alive were high.

BOBBI-BOBBI

The bobbi-bobbi was a giant snake. According to legend, bobbi-bobbi one day realised that humans needed to eat to survive. He sent some flying foxes for men to catch. The men, however, did not know how to hunt. Bobbi-bobbi then sent one of his ribs. The men used the rib as a boomerang to kill the animals. The people later threw the rib up and made a hole in the sky. This angered bobbi-bobbi and he took the rib back and left his people.

Drop bears were thought to resemble koala bears. The legend of the drop bear probably has its roots in a pre-historic creature that looked like koalas but were twice the size

LYCANS

Vampires and werewolves are two of the most enduring legends of our times. Werewolf stories are especially common and are found in many parts of the world. The word 'werewolf' has been derived from the Saxon language and means 'man wolf'.

LYCANTHROPY

The condition describing a person changing into a wolf or any other animal is called lycanthropy. It is also a mental illness that makes the patient believe he has changed into an animal, and he starts to act like one. The most common lycanthrope was that of the werewolf, but there were many other types in which humans were thought to transform into dogs, bears, foxes and leopards – depending on which animal was more common in the specific region. In Polynesia, there even existed legends of the were-shark!

According to some European folklore, a werewolf's true human form could be revealed by throwing a piece of iron over, or at, the werewolf

BIRTH OF THE WEREWOLF

The werewolf legend has one of its earliest origins in Greek mythology. It was probably based on the legend of Lycaon, the king of Arcadia. Lycaon served Zeus the flesh of a child during a feast. Zeus realised what the king had done, and punished him by turning Lycaon into a wolf. Another legend, from Armenia, talked about women who were made to live seven years as a wolf as punishment for their sins. It was believed that a spirit gave such women a wolf skin and told them to put it on. After putting on the skin, a woman was said to first eat her own offspring and then the children of her relatives as well as others in the neighbourhood. She went out only at night and even locked doors could not keep her away, as they opened when she approached. At dawn, the woman changed back into her human form.

THE CURSE OF THE FULL MOON

The transformation into a wolf usually happened during a full-moon night. The werewolf, once fully transformed, was active only at night. It fed on children and dead bodies, and at times even attacked adults. A person could become a werewolf in many ways. One of the easiest ways was to put on a belt or a whole garment made of wolf skin. The person could also rub some magic potion all over the body to turn into a wolf. It was also said that if a woman gives birth to six female children, the seventh child would be a male with the power of changing into a wolf. A person bit by a werewolf would become a werewolf himself. There were many ways to kill the beast. The most common was to use a silver bullet or arrow.

The myth that a werewolf can be killed using a silver bullet is more a work of modern fiction, than of ancient beliefs

SKIN WALKERS

The Navajo Indian tribe of North America believed in a witch called a *yenaldooshi*, who had magical powers to take on the form of a coyote or any other animal. The *yenaldooshi* was said to gain these powers by doing something evil – like killing someone, especially a sibling or one's parents. The *yenaldooshi* wore nothing except a coyote skin. Norse mythology also contained stories of skin walkers. According to the Norse people, a skin walker was able to learn more about an animal or even take on its characteristics by merely wearing the skin of that animal. The most popular skin walker was the berserker. A berserker was a warrior who worshipped the sky god Odin. It was believed that wearing bearskins during battle gave a berserker the strength of a bear.

MAGICAL HORSES

Almost every culture has believed in unicorns and winged horses. Magical hoofed creatures were present in some form in legends told across the world. They usually stood for all that was good and used their magic to help brave men.

UNICORN

The legendary unicorn was known for the spiral horn on its forehead. It was mostly shown as a white horse, but it was also believed to have the beard of a goat and the tail of a lion. The horn, known as alicorn, could heal wounds and act as a cure for poison. The beast was strong and wild, and could not be tamed by man. Only a woman who is pure of heart could capture the unicorn. It was said that when a unicorn came across such a woman in the woods, it would go up to her and lay its head on her lap. Therefore, hunters often used young women as bait. When the woman had put the unicorn to sleep, the hunters came out of their hiding places and cut off its magical horn.

The narwhal, a type of whale, has a spiral, horn-like tooth growing on its head. Experts believe that the single tooth of the narwhals was probably responsible for the legend of the unicorn. In fact, narwhals were at one time hunted extensively for their tooth, which was passed off as a unicorn's horn!

The sea god Poseidon riding on a fish with his son Pegasus, the flying horse, next to him

PEGASUS

In Greek mythology, Pegasus was a flying horse that was born to Poseidon, the god of sea, and Medusa, the gorgon. It was said that when the Greek hero Perseus cut off Medusa's head, Pegasus and his brother Chrysaor the giant sprang from her neck. The winged horse aided Zeus, the king of gods, by carrying his thunderbolts. Pegasus also helped the Greek hero Bellerophon to kill the monster Chimera. Bellerophon later tried to fly to Mount Olympus on the horse, but Pegasus threw him off his back. Bellerophon fell to his death, while Pegasus became a constellation in the sky.

SLEIPNIR

The Norse god Odin's eight-legged horse, Sleipnir, was a magical horse that could travel through air, on land, and over sea. According to Norse mythology, a giant named Blast had offered to rebuild the walls of Asgard destroyed in the war between the Vanirs and the Aesirs. In return, Blast wanted the Sun and the Moon for himself, and the goddess Freya to marry him. Loki the trickster god agreed on the condition that Blast would complete the wall in six months. The giant agreed. Owing to Blast's magical horse Svadilfari, the work proceeded at a fast pace – much to the amazement of the gods. Finally, Loki took on the form of a mare and lured the horse away. The giant became angry and threatened the gods, but the god Thor killed him with his hammer. A few months later, Sleipnir, the child of Loki (disguised as the mare) and Svadilfari, was born. Loki gave the horse to Odin.

The name 'sleipnir' means 'smooth' or 'gliding'. True to its name, the horse Sleipnir was very fast and helped Odin carry souls into the Underworld

CHINESE UNICORN

The Chinese believed in a creature called a qilin. In appearance, the qilin was very different from the unicorn. It was often depicted with a dragon's head, the hooves of an ox, and a pair of horns. Sometimes it was shown with the scales of a fish and the tail of a lion. The qilin was considered to be a good omen. It also punished sinners. The Japanese kirin originated from the qilin, but the former was more deer-like in appearance.

GLOSSARY

Adorn: Decorate

Agate: A stone often used as a semi-precious gemstone

Aesirs: The main gods of the Scandinavians, including Odin, the king of gods; his wife Frigga; and his children, Thor and Baldr, among others

Auspicious: Good omen

Commemorate: Honour the memory of an individual or some event

Confer: To give

Confront: To face

Constellation: A group of stars forming an image of an animal or some object

Depict: To show

Devour: To eat, especially in a greedy manner

Endow: To be given something, or to have an inborn characteristic or talent

Fertility: The condition of being able to conceive and produce offspring

Gnaw: To nibble or bite at something constantly

Guardian: Protector

Gully: A narrow gorge formed by the flow of water in that area

Hideous: Extremely ugly

Hound: dog

Immortality: A state of being able to live forever

Labyrinth: A complicated network of passages that forms a maze

Loch Ness: A lake in Inverness, Scotland

Lure: To attract or to tempt

Meditate: To focus one's mind on something spiritual or holy

Merlin: A legendary sorcerer who was believed to live during King Arthur's time

Mesopotamians: Sumerians, Akkadians, Assyrians and Babylonians were together known as Mesopotamians

Mission: Assignment, task

Mutilate: To injure

Myrrh: A substance obtained from certain trees used in perfumes

Oracle: A Greek priest or priestess who was said to be capable of predicting the future

Personify: To stand for something, or to represent something or someone

Potion: A magical drink

Predict: To state something about the future in advance

Resemble: To look like something or someone else

Resurrection: To be restored to life

Slay: Kill

Sorceress: A female sorcerer, or magician

Spine: Sharp, pointed outgrowth, thorn

Spiritual: Holy

Supreme: Highest authority, or chief

Torso: Upper part of the body from the neck below

Tyr: Scandinavian god of war

Vanirs: The Scandinavians believed in a second group of gods called Vanir. This group included Njord, the god of the sea; his children Freyr and Freya; and others. The Vanirs represented fertility and love

Wattles: The fleshy part of a turkey or a rooster that hangs from the head or the neck

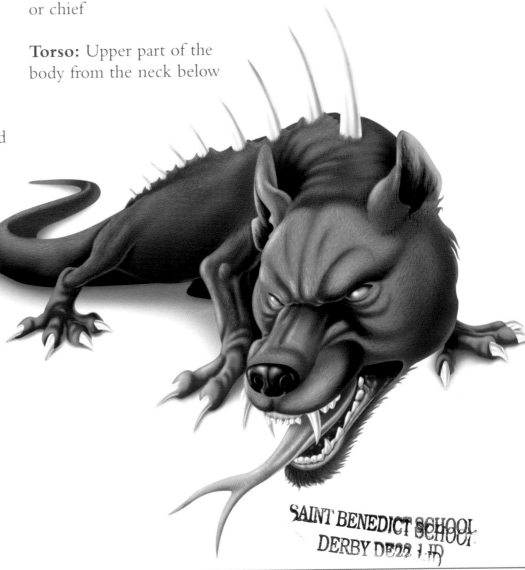